Anger management therapy

How to handle anger issues

NICK HARPER

Table of contents

Introduction

Depending on the listener's familiarity with this feeling, describing someone as "angry" can conjure up various images. They may have an image in their mind of a grumbling granddad, a youngster having a temper tantrum or a colleague who won't give in. These three instances all include the external manifestation of an emotion known as anger, making them all suitable.

Most individuals sometimes experience anger. Many people can also find themselves on the receiving end of individuals who react angrily. The way we respond to anger—whether it's our own or someone else's—can determine whether we're calm or agitated, proactive or reactive, and equanimous or suffering.

A psychotherapeutic approach to controlling and preventing rage is called anger management. It has been said to be an effective use of rage. Often, frustration or feeling stopped or impeded from what the individual believes is vital are the causes of anger.

Ecclesiastes 7:8-10
Solomon contrasts quickly to anger with forbearance. We become upset quickly and often. Often, completing a good job is preferable simply because it has been done properly and does not need further inspection to ensure that the quality of the work was performed. How frequently does someone's temperament affect how well they perform their work and how well they do it? God is unmistakably implying that an individual's disposition has a significant impact on the quality and constancy of his production.

Does a person who is enraged make a good spouse?

Does someone agitated or irritable make a good employee?

Do angry people make excellent churchgoers?

Does a person driving when furious on the road make a good driver?

Anger is often not a sign of intelligence. If anger is utilized appropriately, under control, for the correct reasons, and is not just a reaction to selfish, deliberate annoyance that something is not going the way you intended it to, it may be beneficial. Take note of how the passages that follow demonstrate how anger may thwart good:

Proverbs 14:17: "A quick-tempered man acts foolishly, and a man of wicked intentions is hated."

Proverbs 14:29: "He who is slow to wrath has great understanding, but he who is impulsive exalts folly."

Proverbs 16:32: "He who is slow to anger is better than the mighty, and he who rules his spirit than he who takes a city."

James 1:19-20: "So then, my beloved brethren, let every man be swift to hear, slow to speak, slow to wrath; for the wrath of man does not produce the righteousness of God."

Ecclesiastes 7:9 by Solomon explicitly says, "Anger lies in the heart of idiots."
Because one's pride tells him that even little irritations should not occur to such a beautiful person as he is, he expresses wrath that is ready to erupt at the slightest irritant. His impatience causes him to erupt.

We put off conquering even the smallest character flaws to alter our behavior because we often feel afraid to start. However, we often discover that after engaging in self-discipline and taking a few tentative baby steps, we are encouraged because more good is occurring than we ever imagined. Some minor beginnings have very important finishes.

Chapter 1

Anger.

Anger is a typical human emotion that we all sometimes feel. Like other emotions, rage may serve as a helpful signal that something within us is missing. An immediate, natural reaction to dangers is anger. For us to survive, we need to be angry sometimes. When you struggle to manage your anger, you run the risk of saying or doing something you'll later regret.

Anger may manifest itself in a variety of ways, from little annoyance to ferocious anger. It might be aimed at someone (such as a parent, sibling, neighbor, or total stranger), something (like a delayed train or missed flight), or something else entirely (such as a pair of tangled earphones).

Types Of Anger

Unexpectedly, anger is a complicated feeling. It may occur for a variety of causes and under a variety of conditions. Imagine a sports fan roaring at the television or a mother ignoring her moody teenage daughter as examples of the many ways people might vent their anger. Even the same person reacting differently to the same event at various periods is not uncommon.

Psychologists disagree on the number of types of rage and the best way to categorize them due to these complications. Experts often discuss different ways to convey anger, such as quiet, aggressive, or outspoken.

There are three sorts of rage, and they influence how we respond when something gets us upset. They are assertive anger, open aggression, and passive aggression. Assertive Anger is the finest strategy when you're furious. Check out what each sort of big word implies.

1. Passive aggression

The concept of passive anger, sometimes known as passive-aggressive fury, describes how to manage angry feelings by, well, not managing them. People who express themselves in this way often attempt to contain their emotions and avoid dealing with upsetting circumstances. However, those who use passive aggression still communicate their anger. They often express their rage by being judgemental, circulating stories, or harboring grudges.

2. Outward hostility.

On the other side, many individuals have a propensity to lose control when they are angry or enraged, acting violently or verbally, and often harming themselves or other people. The term for this is open aggression. Fighting, bullying, blackmailing, accusing, yelling, quarreling, sarcasm, and criticism are ways in which this manifests itself. Open hostility comes from a need for control.

3. Aggressive rage.
Being calm and self-assured, speaking and listening, and being willing to assist in handling the problem are all good ways to cope with anger. Relationships may develop as a result of this assertive fury. It entails planning your words before you say them, and being certain in your delivery while being flexible and open to the "other side." It entails exercising patience, keeping your voice down, expressing your emotional state, and attempting to comprehend what others are experiencing.

Causes Of Anger Problems

Anger may be brought on by a variety of causes, such as stress, interpersonal troubles, and money concerns. Some people's anger is a symptom of a deeper illness, such as alcoholism or depression.

Although anger is a recognized symptom of many mental health issues, anger is not considered to be an illness in and of itself.

The following are a few potential triggers for anger management problems.

1. Depression.
Depression is defined by persistent feelings of melancholy and lack of interest that endure for at least two weeks. Anger may be a sign of depression.

Anger may be repressed or outwardly shown. Each individual expresses anger differently, both in terms of intensity and mode of expression.

You can also encounter additional symptoms if you're depressed. These consist of:

Irritability

loss of power

Sense of helplessness

Suicidal or self-harming ideas

2. Compulsive behavior disorder.
Obsessive thoughts and compulsive behaviors are hallmarks of obsessive-compulsive disorder (OCD), an anxiety condition. An OCD sufferer is driven to repeat actions by unwelcome, upsetting thoughts, impulses, or visions.

For instance, individuals could engage in rituals like counting to a specific number or repeating a word or phrase out of a false sense of security that something horrible would happen if they don't.

Research indicated that rage is a prevalent sign of OCD. Approximately 50% of OCD sufferers are affected.

Anger may be a reaction to someone or something interfering with a routine or to irritation over your failure to control obsessive thoughts and compulsive activities.

3. Abuse of alcohol.
According to research, consuming alcohol makes people more aggressive. About half of all violent crimes in the United States include alcohol as a significant component. Alcohol abuse, often known as alcoholism, is the frequent or excessive use of alcohol.

Alcohol reduces your capacity for clear thinking and logical decision-making. You may find it more difficult to manage your emotions and it may impact your ability to resist impulses.

4. Attention deficit hyperactivity syndrome.
Inattention, hyperactivity, and/or impulsivity are some of the symptoms of

attention deficit hyperactivity disorder (ADHD), a neurodevelopmental condition.

Early childhood is the typical time for the onset of symptoms, which lasts the rest of a person's life. Some individuals might not get a diagnosis for ADHD until they are adults, a condition is known as adult ADHD. People with ADHD of all ages might also experience anger and irritability. Additional signs include:

Restlessness.

Difficulties concentrating.

Inadequate planning or time management abilities

5. Oppositional defiant disorder.
A behavioral problem called oppositional defiant disorder (ODD) affects 1 to 16 percent of school-age children. ODD symptoms often include:

Anger

Rapid temper

Irritability

ODD children often become quickly irritated by other people. They could be combative and stubborn.

6. Bipolar illness.
A brain illness called bipolar disorder may cause abrupt mood changes. Though not everyone with the bipolar disease may suffer melancholy, these abrupt mood swings can range from mania to it. Anger, impatience, and fury episodes are common among persons with bipolar illness.

They might: During a manic episode,

Be prone to agitation.

Feel ecstatic.

Having frenzied thoughts.

Pose impulsive or risky actions.

You might: During a depressed episode:

Feel depressed, defeated, or crying.

A loss of interest in once-enjoyed activities.

Have suicidal thoughts.

7. Periodic exploding disorder.
Intermittent explosive disorder (IED) is characterized by recurrent bouts of aggressive, impulsive, or violent conduct. They could overreact to events by having irrational, uncalled-for furious outbursts.

Less than 30-minute episodes start at random and last for a short time. People who have the condition may often feel irritated and furious.

Several typical actions

Anger outbursts.

Arguments.

Fighting.

Physical abuse.

Hurling objects.

After an incident, those with IEDs may feel regretful or ashamed.

8. Grief

One of the phases of grieving is anger. Grief might be from a loved one's passing, a divorce or breakup, or losing your job. The individual who passed away, anybody else engaged in the incident, or inanimate things may be the targets of the rage. Other sorrow signs and symptoms include:

Shock.

Numbness.

Guilt.

Sadness.

Loneliness.

Fear.

Chapter 2

Know your triggers.

Like every other emotion, we experience every day, anger is a normal feeling. We may get upset at any moment about any issue, person, or thought. Children and adults both experience rage for the same reasons.

Anger triggers may be divided into two categories.

1. Internal Triggers.

2. External Triggers.

As the name imply, two elements affect how much rage we feel in a given day or instant. Triggers might be thoughts, events, people, locations, or objects that are connected to binge drinking or drug usage.

1. Internal triggers.
The emotions that one feels within are known as triggers. They are not defined by their environment or surroundings. There are several feelings or circumstances that we go through that might make us furious. For instance, you can get irate if you feel guilty about not being liked by someone. Another circumstance where we might see youngsters becoming angry is when someone else does better than you do in academics. When you are the only one engaged in a scenario like this, we often feel irritated.

2. External triggers.
The outside stimuli that irritate us make up for external triggers. Even though anger is a natural feeling that we all experience, certain situations make us angry. For instance, you received an unwarranted

smack. In such a circumstance, anger is inevitable.

Alcohol or drug misuse are other outside influences that might make someone angry. All of a person's emotions are elevated by the use of such drugs. It explains why someone who is intoxicated fights more forcefully than someone sober.

How can you recognize your triggers?

The inability to comprehend what is amplifying their triggers is a difficulty shared by all individuals with anger management problems. Understanding the source of your anger and taking steps to address it are crucial components of anger management if you want to prevent irrational, uncontrollable rage.

However, if a person is unable to comprehend the source of their rage, they are unsure of how to control it. We can readily comprehend what sets us off and what makes us feel peaceful if we pay attention to our emotional patterns. Here are several indicators to help you assess and comprehend your triggers in case you're nonetheless perplexed.

List of external triggers

The triggers that occur outside of you are known as external triggers. You become furious more often because of something that someone else said or did. However, you don't become irritated or hostile as a result of external causes. They just increase your likelihood of being irate. You may choose how you wish to react and respond to such stimuli.

1. Someone disagreed with what I said: Let's face it, these days, everyone wants the other person to accept and obey their choice. Being an entrepreneur, I often see individuals who merely want their ideas to

be put into action. Often, we become so self-centered that we purposefully disagree with others, even though their view is superior to our own. When we believe someone is not on our side, we get enraged.

2. Someone made fun of me: People are not always nice in all circumstances. When someone feels insecure or jealous, they often ridicule and mock that person. They may or might not be purposely teasing you, but it is clear how you would respond. When someone makes fun of you, you will get enraged, and it is only normal that your rage would manifest itself in some way. Mark it as a trigger if someone making fun of you makes you feel triggered.

3. You erred; errors are something we all do. While some errors are minor, greater errors may sometimes occur. Some errors might have unfavorable results and leave you feeling defenseless. We feel upset with ourselves when we screw up. Such that we

lower ourselves in the process. Take the case when you fail to pay the power bill by the deadline. You're going to be furious with yourself. It demonstrates how making a mistake makes you angry.

4. I was picked on: People aren't very friendly to one another nowadays. They often target those who are simple prey. Your coworkers, classmates, or college pals could continually make fun of you. Sometimes, a person turns into their preferred objective, which begins to worry them. Your anger will be aroused if someone consistently irritates you or makes you feel awful. The only solution is to stay as far away from them as you can, rather than hurling insults at them.

5. Someone exploited my possessions: Many individuals desire to maintain their privacy. They don't meddle too much in other people's affairs, and they hold others to the same standard. On the other side, some individuals like giving and supporting

others. Now, it irritates them to no end when someone utilizes their private property. They get enraged and accuse the other person of violating their privacy. Using anything as simple as their face cleanser is enough to make them angry. They may feel rage within themselves, whether or not they express it to you.

6. I saw the person I didn't like: I believe that in such circumstances, we all have triggers. We get irritated whenever we see someone we don't like or who has wronged us. We get enraged out of the blue. Simply seeing someone's face makes us angry. It may be an ex, your employer, or a member of your family. It seems to me that it is the simplest method to attribute your feelings to someone else. "Usko dekh liya, toh din bura gya" comes naturally to us. When I saw his face, my whole day turned out badly. The simplest trigger for everyone is encountering or conversing with someone you don't like.

7. They ignored me: When someone ignores us, we often experience anxiety and rage. Human nature is at its most fundamental. We get enraged at others if we see that they are being impolite to us or are ignoring us. For instance, you may run into a buddy of yours at a mall. He glances at you before ignoring you. You'll be so furious that you won't speak to him for a few days. Even though ignorance might make people angry, fury is uncontrollable. You can't make anybody avoid you.

List of internal triggers

Internal triggers take place in your mind. An internal trigger is a notion that surfaces after an event or after meeting someone. It is the outcome of a "Self-Talk," to be exact.

1. I'll impart a lesson to him or her: How often do you use it? Isn't it the case a lot? No one now wants to accept stupidity or listen

to it. In numerous circumstances in life, we must deal with various sorts of individuals. While some individuals are giving and helpful, others could just be here to further their interests. For instance, you had a buddy that you admired. She only needed your support while she moved on, and once she did, she decided to leave you. You now have two choices: either you'll accept and go on, or you won't. The alternative is to exact retribution, which is always motivated by wrath. You would reflect on everything that you had done for someone and how they had abandoned you in the process. It has to do with how you internally make yourself angry.

2. He or she ought not to have acted that way: I usually maintain that you have no control over what the people around you do. No matter how hard you try, you cannot control what the outside world does to you, I constantly tell my clients. Some individuals are impolite and will never treat anybody

with respect. Either you can unleash your fury on them or you can simply let it go. You know you've pushed your anger button when you think, "She shouldn't press my buttons like that." Although you have no control over what another person does to you, you can always choose how you will respond.

3. He's deliberately doing it: It makes me think of a recent occurrence. A few days ago, a furious employee of my organization approached me. I questioned him about what was wrong and his excessive rage. He said that the presentation, which had taken him three days to prepare, had been removed. I asked him if he knew who did it or how it occurred because I was horrified. I'm quite confident Xyz (another employee) did it, he stated right away. I inquired as to what motivated his viewpoint. He said that he always envies his success and seeks for methods to undermine me. I requested that

the management group look into the matter to see whether it was the case. It turned out, however, that he neglected to save the file himself.

What I'm trying to express is that most of the time, we act out of rage because we believe that someone intentionally wronged us. We become upset for days after we believe anything was done to bother you on purpose.

4. I'm not going to let her off the hook for this: Ah! Retribution is the most rewarding emotion of all. What she did to me, I ought to do to her. Today's youth adheres to the tit-for-tat philosophy. When someone wrongs us, we try to find methods to hurt them even more. This trigger solely relies on a person's mindset. Many individuals choose to let go of these circumstances. Some individuals, however, would go over and above to prevent the other person from getting away with what they did. Crime rates

in the nation have increased due to this raging problem.

5. It is unfair: Since we were little children, we have developed the habit of comparing what we get to what others receive. You used to become upset about the unfair choice when someone else received two chocolates while you only received one. You will then blatantly claim that someone made an unjust choice, which is why you were outraged. In contrast, fury was a feeling that manifested itself.

Chapter 3

Symptoms of anger issues.

Anger is a typical human emotion that may be advantageous in some circumstances, such as in response to threats of danger or injury to oneself or others. However, uncontrolled anger may become destructive, lead to issues in your life, and have a bad impact on your personal and professional relationships.

It's crucial to recognize the symptoms of rage difficulties and comprehend how to deal with them. This guards you against deterioration of your mental health, physical troubles, and marital concerns. Our health is severely harmed by anger. A person who is always furious can never be in perfect health. Our physical health is strongly impacted by stress and rage.

What are some outward manifestations of anger?

1. Verbal Outbursts of Rage
Outbursts are common among people with anger management problems. As a kind of mental health illness, anger may worsen and include abrupt outbursts of violence, impulsivity, or disruptive conduct. When you have anger management problems, you may accidentally smash things, hurt people or animals, get angry on the road a lot, or have temper tantrums. This has a bad impact on your relationships, job, and academics. Additionally, it can have legal repercussions.

Typically, aggressive outbursts are accompanied by:

Irate conduct.

Becomes overexcited or hyper.

Quickly becomes agitated.

Hurried thoughts.

Shaking.

Tingling.

A complaint of heart discomfort.

Rapid breathing or palpitations.

Explosive verbal and physical outbursts may be expressed via berating, slapping, shoving, heated debates, physical battles, property destruction, and assaults on people or animals.

2. You sense that something is wrong.
Various sexes may exhibit different forms of anger difficulties. The same holds at various ages. View the examples below to see if you

can identify with any of the warning indicators of anger management issues:

You often instigate fights.

You constantly assign blame.

You maintain that your actions are acceptable because others around you are overly sensitive. The brain now tries to explain away the undesirable behavior.

You have a hard time expressing your feelings, except for becoming furious to regain some control.

Your aggressive actions give you the impression that you can dominate others.

When you're around, you notice that your friends, family, or coworkers seem uneasy or as if they're treading water.

When you lose control of your rage, you inadvertently harm other individuals.

3. Constantly Troubled By the Past

Imagine if your errors and failures from the past kept coming back to mind. If that's the case, you'll probably feel disappointed in yourself. You may get more irate if you have ongoing grudges and are constantly annoyed by other individuals or situations.

4. Irritable

The opposite of bitterness and despair is happiness. Long-term sadness may be torturous for your loved ones as much as for you. Because individuals achieve momentary satisfaction or euphoria in these damaging practices, some people resort to them. Examples include drug misuse, drunkenness, and smoking.

5. Breathing Quickly

Shallow breathing is often seen as a telltale indicator of anger. Do breathing exercises if you start to feel short of breath. Your body's fight-or-flight mechanism, which is activated by anger, releases the hormone adrenaline. You may relax your body by practicing deep breathing.

Other symptoms.

Heartbeat quickens.

Your body may feel stiff or have tight muscles.

Sweating is a common sign of anger. You will perspire more than other individuals if you are under a lot of stress or are still upset.

A dry mouth is another symptom of rage in the body. The majority of persons who struggle with rage often notice little salivation.

Another very frequent adverse impact of rage is stomach problems. After expressing rage, you'd often have some stomach issues.

The person's fists are among the most frequent physical indicators of fury. When we are angry with someone, we often make a fist.

One extremely frequent negative outcome of rage is sickness.

An angry scenario usually sticks with you. You repeatedly replay the same argument or circumstance in your thoughts, which makes you even more irate.

Another indicator of rage is sweating beneath the arms or clenching your fists.

Chapter 4

Anger management In personal relationships and the workplace.

Anger Management In Personal Relationships.

Relationships, especially romantic ones, but also ones with friends and family members, are often characterized by anger. Although it is common, we often are unaware of the underlying nature of this strong feeling or how it affects our loved ones. Understanding how relationships are affected by anger may help you better manage your anger or deal with an angry spouse, friend, or family member.

There are several kinds of anger. Not every manifestation of this feeling has a target. For instance, rage that is unfocused due to bereavement and annoyance with your laptop is not targeted. Targetless rage may be problematic in relationships, yet it often results in disagreements that are simple to resolve.

Hostile anger, as opposed to anger without a specific target, may worsen marital issues since it is associated with responsibility and blame. Hostile fury is sometimes referred to as "rage" or "wrath" in its most evil forms. Fury fits or outbursts are common manifestations of angry anger that dissipates fast.

The frequency and severity of rage outbursts determine the effects of short-lived anger on a relationship. Verbal, emotional, or physical abuse may take the shape of recurrent, high-intensity outbursts. They consist of shouting, calling people names, making derogatory remarks, threatening people, punching walls, slamming doors, hurling things, and striking.

However, not all rage is fleeting. Because certain marital difficulties have never been addressed and resolved, anger may sometimes persist. When anger persists, it transforms into resentment or outrage.

We respond to a supposedly unfair situation in both bitterness and fury. When we are resentful, we believe the person we are resenting has done us personally wrong. In relationships, resentment often develops when we believe the other person has treated us unfairly or wrongly—and not simply by accident. For instance, if a close friend of yours invites almost everyone else except you to their wedding, this might cause long-lasting bitterness against the buddy.

The vicarious equivalent of resentment is indignation, or what we sometimes refer to as "outrage." When you are angry, an injustice committed against another person—possibly a societal wrong—is what you are worried about. Even if outrage might arise for good reasons, if it is not communicated or controlled properly, this kind of rage can nonetheless endanger our relationships.

For instance, you could be outraged to find that your mother, an R&D director at a large organization, just took a 50% increase although her employer just let 200 of its employees go. Because of the outrage, you feel in this situation, you can later come to believe your mother is a nasty person, turning your resentment into hate or disdain. Even the start of the breakdown of your formerly tight parental connection might result from deep-seated resentment against your mother.

Emotional abuse, particularly passive-aggressive techniques like the silent treatment, communicating in codes, attempting to win sympathy, repeated amnesia, or morose conduct, to mention a few, may also result from deep-seated bitterness and outrage. So how can we control and deal with rage problems in relationships? Here are some pointers.

1. Be mindful of your words.
To wait a moment before responding is one of the greatest strategies. Stop shouting at your buddy, relative, or the person who just drove in front of you in traffic if your heart is racing and you feel like it. Breathe in deeply. Take all necessary precautions to prevent snapping and saying or doing anything you'll later regret.

2. When you are at ease, explain what disturbed you.

Be forceful yet non-confrontational in how you express your anger. Perhaps after you cooked supper, your partner didn't help clean the kitchen. Or maybe your kid took your vehicle and once again returned it with almost little petrol left. Use an "I" statement to clearly and concisely express your worries. Say something like, "I'm angry that you didn't give me enough petrol to drive to work," or "I dislike when I labor to make dinner and you don't help clean up afterward."

3. Laugh it off to reduce stress.

Laughter may assist reduce stress. Use humor to help you confront the things that are upsetting you and, maybe, any irrational expectations you may have about how things should turn out. Sarcasm should be avoided, however, since it might irritate others and worsen the situation.

4. Have a break.
Not just timeouts for children. During difficult moments of the day, allow yourself brief pauses. You could feel more equipped to manage what is ahead without becoming upset or furious if you have a few quiet minutes to yourself.

5. Take a workout.
Exercise may aid in reducing stress, which can make you furious. If you see that your anger is growing, engage in some fun physical activity, such as a quick walk or run.

6. Work on your relaxation abilities.
Try deep breathing exercises, visualize a soothing environment, or repeat a word or phrase that is comforting, such as "Take it easy." You may utilize yoga and meditation as effective calming techniques. It's simpler to handle the difficulties life presents you with when you take care of yourself.

7. Don't harbor resentment.
It is a strong instrument to forgive. You risk being overcome by your resentment or sense of unfairness if you let anger and other negative emotions overpower happy ones. However, you may both grow from the experience and improve your relationship if you can forgive the person who offended you.

8. List potential answers
Work on fixing the problem at hand rather than dwelling on the thing that enraged you. Are you angry about your child's filthy room? Knock on the door. Every night, does your spouse arrive late for dinner? Plan your meals for later in the day. Or decide to eat alone a couple of times each week. Additionally, be aware that certain circumstances are just beyond your control. Regarding what you can and cannot alter, try to be practical. Remind yourself that

becoming angry won't help and can even make things worse.

Handling of anger at workplace

When anything is said or done at work, anger might be expressed as sentiments of irritation, resentment, or discontent. Frequently, occurrences like unhappiness with corporate policy, strict deadlines, or an unbalanced workload are to blame. You can control your anger, however, and contribute to a constructive change in the workplace.

What advantages can restraining your rage at work provide?

Employees may feel more comfortable communicating and interacting with one another at work if there is less anger there. If anger is not controlled, it often shows itself as increased staff absences and low morale. You may follow a strategy for coping with unpleasant emotions if you know how to direct your anger in a more constructive direction. You may identify ideas to assist enhance your working environment by getting together with others to talk about how an event impacts you.

The benefits of managing your rage at work are as follows:

Helps you express your demands and takes care of them.

Enhances interactions with customers and employees.

Reduces anxiety and other unpleasant feelings.

Eliminates emotions and signs related to rage.

Minimizes workplace distractions and improves your ability to concentrate on your activities.

Enhances performance and productivity.

Prevents the occurrence of passive aggression.

Aids in preventing harmful getaways or addictive behaviors.

Increases empathy among employees.

How to control your emotions while you're upset at work.

Follow these instructions to control your emotions when you get irritated at work:

1. Recognize your rage.
Look into the root of your anger to see what is creating it. There could often be a real problem at work that you can examine to assist in resolving. Always keep in mind that rage is a typical feeling and your body's response to a "threat." It's beneficial to

admit your anger to prevent holding onto it. Examine your anger to determine whether it makes sense in light of the situation.

2. Take a deep breath

Take a few deep breaths to help you relax when you start to feel angry. Exercises that deepen breathing might help your brain relax and divert your focus from your anger. You might also try counting to ten, reciting a soothing mantra, or using your favorite music as a diversion.

3. Speak to a reliable person.

Tell a trustworthy person what happened that caused you to feel furious. They may be able to provide you with information or advice that you didn't consider and help you understand why you feel the way you do. To protect your privacy, you should be cautious about with whom you disclose information and talk. Look for someone who can listen well and has empathy.

4. Take a break.
To get away from the situation that made you angry, leave the office or job. To focus your energies on something more productive, go for a little stroll. Consider the problem and potential solutions during this period. This could make it easier for you to remain composed and address the issue from a new angle.

5. Take into account how a person you respect might respond to this scenario.
To get fresh insight, consider how your role model or supervisor might respond to this circumstance. Consider how they may react if you could imagine them in your shoes. To avoid reacting poorly by using behaviors like yelling, try visualizing how a respected person would handle anger.

6. Speak with the persons involved about your anger.
Set up a meeting with the persons involved in the circumstance that incited your rage

after you have cooled down and can think more clearly. Consider bringing in a third person to act as a mediator during the meeting, depending on the state of your relationship with the person. Avoid placing blame while talking to the other person since it could make them want to defend themselves or launch a counterattack. Instead, try determining what is required to proceed, coming to an understanding while keeping the aim in mind, and moving ahead.

7. Create a strategy of action

Specify the actions to be taken to remediate the trigger occurrence. Find answers if the source of your rage is something you can alter. However, if it involves anything beyond your control, work on changing your attitude and learning to accept the way things are. When you let things go, your physical health is no longer impacted by your anger.

8. Put your happiness first
While there may be aspects of your job that are beyond your control, you can choose how you react to the situation. To improve your experience and produce more effective work, try to be more upbeat at work.

Conclusion

More tips on anger management

1. Determine your triggers.

If you want to reduce the frequency and intensity of angry outbursts in your life, start by keeping a careful eye on the people, places, and situations that often set you off. You may not be able to avoid these triggers, and you shouldn't try to get rid of everything that gives you a little anxiety, but you can start making plans for them. For instance, it would be worthwhile to leave the home an hour sooner and have a stress-free journey to work with much less traffic if you discover that you arrive at work in a cranky mood most days because you spent too much time in traffic concerned you would be late. You could also want to utilize your understanding of your particular triggers to calm yourself before potentially upsetting events by practicing anger management methods like deep breathing.

2. Take note of your anger's outward manifestations.

Anger causes bodily responses, just like any other strong emotion. You could have seen these signs before you realized you had an anger issue, or you might still be completely oblivious of them. You may halt anger in its tracks or recover as quickly after an outburst by paying attention to the bodily symptoms of impending wrath as well as how you feel during and after an episode of rage. Although every person's relationship between body and mind is unique, some universal warning signs of mounting rage include feeling heated, having a quick heartbeat, trembling, and clenched fists. When you find yourself on a disastrous course, being able to recognize your body's physical response to triggers might help you deliberately shift course.

3. Locate a constructive diversion

We often relive both actual and imagined events in our brains when we are highly upset with someone or something, which exacerbates our emotions and makes it challenging to think sensibly. Find a healthy diversion as your finest option for keeping your attention off devouring emotions. Physical or creative hobbies keep us rooted in the present and prevent us from daydreaming, making them the perfect diversions. To find a constructive outlet for your emotions, try going for a run or engaging in some art therapy. You could even discover that after clearing your head, you can handle problems more effectively.

4. Ascertain the origin of your feelings.

The best course of action often is seeking expert assistance while trying to eradicate troublesome anger from your life. Finding the root causes of your anger may need counseling or anger management training, but none of these options will help you regulate your thoughts and behavior. Living in chronic rage may harm your relationships, work, and health by increasing your chances of diabetes, high blood pressure, and heart disease. Determine if your anger is a result of current circumstances that need to be changed, unresolved emotional problems, mental illness, or prior trauma with the aid of professional therapy. Anger is often a coping technique for extreme anxiety or a protection mechanism to keep you from being exposed to relationship misery. You may endeavor to create a better, more serene existence for yourself and the people around you by learning to decode your emotions.